YOU GOT IN!!

EssaySnark's Post-Admit Business School Prep Guide

YOU GOT IN!!

EssaySnark's Post-Admit Business School Prep Guide

by EssaySnark®

Snarkolicious Press

Paperback edition
originally published January 31, 2014
version 1.1 February 3, 2014

Snarkolicious Press
P. O. Box 50021
Palo Alto, CA 94303

www.snarkoliciouspress.com

978 1 938098 18 5

"Now this is not the end. It is not even the beginning of the end. But it is, perhaps, the end of the beginning."

Winston Churchill

About This *SnarkStrategies Guide*

CONGRATULATIONS, BRAVE SUPPLICANT! YOU MADE IT INTO BSCHOOL!

You're probably still celebrating – and you should be! This alone is a major accomplishment.

You worked hard. GMAT. Essays. Maybe GMAT again. Recommendations and applications and interviews. And you did it!

Whether you were admitted in the first round or the last one, in your first try or only after many attempts as a reapplicant, you're headed to bschool in a number of months. And you're probably not ready for it in the slightest.

This *SnarkStrategies Guide* will offer up some to-dos and tasks and basic projects that you'll need to undertake at some point in your near-term pre-matriculation future – many of which you've likely already thought of, others perhaps you haven't.

This is not meant to be a replacement to all the great information that your school will make available to you once you pay your deposit and become official. However, you may not even be in a position yet where you can make that deposit payment; it's possible that you're now in the completely awesome position of having to choose between multiple offers. We'll offer some advice on navigating that enviable yet difficult situation.

We'll also tell you what to expect in the realms of:

- Financial matters – when you'll need to start paying for what

- Academic matters – what knowledge and skillsets you should be equipped with before stepping foot in your first MBA classroom

- Personal matters – challenges you may not realize you'll be facing with this big life transition

- Logistical matters – issues that you should anticipate in planning your move to your new city

- International matters – foreign students have a lot to handle in relocating to another country, yet domestic students should also plan ahead for the likelihood of international travel during their MBA experience

This *SnarkStrategies Guide* is primarily geared towards incoming students matriculating at American business schools, though much of the advice is still relevant if you're headed to, say, the UK to go to LBS, or Spain to go to IE or ESADE or one of those other great schools, etc. It's also focused on the challenges and concerns faced by the soon-to-be full-time student – in other words, those of you who are quitting your jobs and uprooting your lives to move to some new place to attend school for two years. It's less suitable to a part-time or local EMBA candidate, though some of it may apply to those types of students, too.

Here's the email exchange with a successful Brave Supplicant that inspired us to write this guide:

On Thu, Jan 12, 2012 at 10:52 AM, Brave Supplicant wrote:

LOL these are perfect for me!

I was sitting at dinner last night and the full weight of $100k+ of tuition plus living expenses hit me, but I didn't let that bring me down at all and I'm still overly excited.

Maybe there should be a:

HowToActLikeYouAreStillFocusedAtWork.com or something.

On Thu, Jan 12, 2012 at 10:40 AM, Essay Snark wrote:
> Hey Brave Supplicant! Probably the most frequented post-admissions sites are things like:
>
> - 108 Ways to Tell Your Boss to Blow Off
> - the *OMGHowAmIGonnaAffordThisThing* blog
> and
> - ExoticDestinations.com
>
> :-)
>
> We'll see if we can think up some more, uh, PRACTICAL sites for ya soon!
>
> EssaySnark
>
>
>
> On Thu, Jan 12, 2012 at 8:45 AM, BraveSupplicant wrote:
>>
>> ES,
>>
>> Sorry for blowing up your e-mail, but I have a quick question for you. My usual 'coffee and blog check' now seems moot as every morning I would check places like Accepted, ClearAdmit, etc just to get more tips on the application process and all that good stuff. I will probably still go to those places (after ES of course!) but I was wondering if you had any suggestions for sites to visit more geared to starting the transition? My girlfriend is excited for the "What to Expect When You Are Expecting" movie and I wish there was something like that for b-school. "What to Assume When you are Admitted?" doesn't have quite the same ring, but you get the gist.
>>
>> Any suggestions?
>>
>> Thanks!
>>
>> Brave Supplicant

Maybe the full weight of this proposition has started to hit you, too. We're here to help! We can't promise to cover every little facet of every little decision you'll have to make in the coming months, but we'll help you anticipate the big ones and see what you'll be up against. You now have all the resources of a great bschool to help you out, and you should obviously turn to them for answers and support along the way.

If you come across any situations that you think should be covered in this *Guide* which we've missed, it would be great if you'd let us know! Or, if you have a pre-matriculation bschool readiness question that you think we can help with, we'd be happy to give it a shot. Drop on over to our blahg at http://essaysnark.com or email us at gethelpnow@essaysnark.com – or even tweet us – and we'll see what we can do to help out.

Table of Contents

First: Money. Expect to Spend Some. Soon.

We're going to be dedicating a whole section of this *Guide* to finances but right here at the beginning, we're going to start with a heads-up. What should hopefully be obvious to you is that getting an MBA is expensive – and for most of you, you won't have any income while you're in school. Lots of money out with no money in can make for a stressful situation.

Even if you read no further in this *Guide*, we hope that you'll take this advice to heart: START SAVING YOUR MONEY NOW. You have a job. Make the most of it.

It is not easy to go from a cush salary and a regular paycheck to the screeching halt (financially) of student-dom. In fact, this is going to be a difficult transition for some of you. Living on zero income is not easy. You'll want to get ready for this – not just in building up a nest egg now, so that you have more flexibility in how you get to live during your two years of bschool, but also some mental preparation so that you're emotionally ready for it.

Most bschool students have been out on their own for at least several years and have gotten accustomed to regular happy hours and a daily Starbucks habit. These things add up. If you've been working as a consultant pre-MBA, then you probably have had a decently liberal expense account policy, and you may be used to living less than frugally. During these next few months of preparation, you should start to pay attention to your lifestyle and how you spend – what sums of money are going out of the bank account every month – and you should consider ratcheting down on the non-essentials, and stashing some cash in savings.

You'll also have some near-term bills to pay as part of the ramp-up to your MBA opening day:

- fees for a background check (mandatory at some schools as part of the final admissions process – usually less than $100)

- deposit(s) to hold your spot in the entering class

- if you're an international student, fees for a visa application (about $200) and possibly notary fees for documents required for that ($20 or so)

- travel costs to attend your school's Admit Weekend – or maybe multiple schools' weekends, if you're trying to decide between offers

- the deposit for your new apartment

- fees to ship your stuff and/or to put it in storage, if your parents' garage is full

- the miscellaneous expenses required in furnishing a new home in a new city

- a one-way plane ticket for the final move to school

- a new laptop if needed

- new clothes if you're moving to a new climate (tip: buy them at the destination)

This is not an exhaustive list. Those categories alone could easily add up to $15,000 or more; at minimum it's like $6,000. If you don't have spare cash like that laying around, you'll need to start looking at where the money is going to come from, pronto. Expect to be hit up for random and miscellaneous fees and charges on a regular basis from now till the start of school. And don't forget to budget for the fun stuff. We didn't even mention pre-MBA travel like Kellogg's Kwest or any vacations that you'll plan on your own to celebrate your freedom. Those are important, too.

You'll also need to get your first year tuition together. That's usually financed through student loans, which we also discuss further on in this *Guide.* Your school has probably already provided you with due dates and requirements for deposits and all that. We simply want to get you thinking about the reality that you're going to have an increase in expenses, starting very soon, and that you'll soon be facing a decrease in income. Get real about this. Bschool is hella fun; financial stress is not. If you're not independently wealthy, start planning your financial life for the next few years now.

Along the lines of "how to prepare" for bschool, we have our first important bit of advice for you:

Get a copy of your credit report. Do this now.

You may be thinking, "Wait, EssaySnark, what does my credit report have to do with anything? And why is this the first thing you're telling me to do?"

The reason you need to get your credit report is that you need to see if there are any errors on it. It wouldn't hurt to also get your FICO score (the FICO score is the number between 300 and 850 that encapsulates the credit bureaus' assessment of your credit worthiness based on a proprietary formula developed by the Fair Isaacs Company). If you're a US citizen, you can get one free credit report a year from each of the three major credit bureaus: Experian, Equifax, and TransUnion. Ideally you'd get a copy from each one, since they can have different data, and it's possible that only one has an error that the others don't. Be careful about signing up for extra services; there's lots of scams and shady companies out there that are charging for credit reports. You don't need to pay for this and you shouldn't even need to submit a credit card number in order to get your free report.

If your credit report shows mistakes, then you'll want to work to resolve those as soon as you can. This process can take considerable time. That's why we advise you to do it now.

The reason? Because your credit report will be accessed in at least one important step of your bschool enrollment process, and possibly multiple steps:

1. If you're going to apply for student loans to finance your education, then the lenders will pull your credit report

2. If your school requires a background check, then the verification service *might* access your credit report

3. When you go to lease an apartment in your new city, then the landlord or realty company will pull your credit report

4. If you decide to buy a car locally at bschool and you get a loan for that, then another credit report will be required

5. If you get a cell phone plan in the US or set up utilities at your new apartment, your credit will be checked

Having decent credit will help you throughout this transition to bschool. You should know what's on that credit report, *now*. Get started on clearing up any errors you find, and if your payment record has been spotty with your current debt obligations, then make a vow to yourself to fix that pattern immediately. Pay off those credit card bills and work to make yourself debt-free before you head to bschool in the fall.

If you're an international student, you may be scratching your head on all this. You won't have a credit report if you've never had any credit in the US. You'll want to change that as soon as possible. Towards the end of this *Guide* we have some suggestions for international students who will be setting up a life in America for the first time. An advance tip? Get an American Express card if you can do so from your home country.

But we may be getting ahead of ourselves. Did you even decide which school you're going to yet?

Deciding on a School (Multiple Offers)

If you already know where you're going for your MBA, lucky you! You can skip this section.

If you have the great good fortune to have received multiple offers and are now faced with the challenges of abundance, then read on.

We've covered a variety of scenarios for people faced with this situation on the EssaySnark blahg; in fact, every year we seem to write a new series of posts on the subject. To find them all, go to essaysnark.com and using the Categories dropdown menu at the top right of the home page, choose "deciding on a school (multiple offers)". The posts discuss the dilemmas involved with choosing a lower-ranked school that's offering a significant scholarship over a "better" one with no money.

Our best advice on how to decide?

Attend the Welcome Weekends of both schools.

Hopefully you've already visited the schools that have accepted you, but if not, now's the time. While both the schools you're considering are likely to be super impressive with great people, we predict that one of them will "speak" to you more than the other(s). That's what Brave Supplicants report to us over and over through the years; they just get a better feeling at one school and they come to realize that it's where they belong. Trust your gut on this stuff.

Here's what one person wrote to us after attending two Admit Weekends:

> In other news admit weekend at School A was AWESOME so I'm definitely going there! I was kind of upset that after School B's admit weekend I was still missing that "this feels right" feeling, so it was such a huge relief to find that I truly did get that feeling this weekend in [city]. I met such impressive, humble, down-to-earth, friendly, fun people, and I couldn't imagine myself not there in [city] with them in the fall. So phew, decision made! And I'm so excited about it!

And here's a report from someone else who was surprised by what they learned after visiting Ross:

> I was extremely impressed during Super Saturday. The building is beautiful, and the people are just fantastic--can't be beat. I initially wanted an urban campus because I wanted to be in a city, but after visiting, I can see how nice a college town can be. The administration also seems really good...I liked how transparent the process was and how friendly the AdCom was. I think MAP is also amazing and wish it was part of every school's curriculum. Ross went from being my "safety" school to quite possibly one of my favorites.

Talk to people to find out their opinions – but be careful about talking to too many. Everyone's got their own ideas and perspectives,but it's YOU who will be going to one of these schools. Listen to what others have to say, but don't get too caught up in what everyone else thinks. No matter if your family and friends are saying that you should do X, if you feel better about Y, then keep your wits about you and stay strong and go with those instincts. It would truly suck to make a decision on which school to go to based on someone else's idea of what's best for you. Stick to your guns.

When weighing options, there are some additional points that you need to know about:

Any school that has accepted you really wants you to enroll.

This may come as a surprise. After the grueling experience of the application process, where you were the Brave Supplicant and may have felt like you were practically groveling at the adcom's feet to get them to admit you, then you may be shocked at how things have changed. The schools are courting you! It may even feel like you're dealing with a different organization now. It's funny how the tables turn once you've been accepted. You can expect the schools to be very welcoming and even more friendly to you than they ever were before, when you were a lowly applicant.

Why is that? Because they care whether you accept their offer or not. All the schools admit more applicants than they have space for, because they know that not everyone will end up enrolling. They want to maximize the numbers who do. The percentage of accepted applicants who say "yes" to them is called their "yield" and it's an important datapoint that they track closely; it even gets factored into their rankings with several of the leading publications. Once you're accepted, you can expect there to be a whole parade of people contacting you for various things, some of them who will be explicitly trying to help you make the decision to choose this school for your MBA.

If you have multiple offers, then you definitely need to continue your research – and you should also be leveraging the additional school resources now available to you. If you have questions about post-MBA employment, for example, feel free to contact the Career Services office. Maybe you contacted them before, during your application process, which would have been totally appropriate – but maybe when you contact them now and identify yourself as an accepted applicant, they could be even more forthcoming and helpful. They might hook you up with some alumni in your field of interest, for example, or they could invite you to campus to sit in on some conference or industry event. You never know. Most people report that the level of warmth and receptivity changes radically once their status goes from "applicant" to "admitted."

That being said, you don't want to push your luck. If you're debating which school to go to, you can't expect the schools themselves to offer any flexibility on their policies.

Case in point:

Deposits are non-refundable, and deposit due dates are non-negotiable.

The schools know that many people get multiple offers – and they know that many people are put on waitlists for other schools. They design their deposit due dates with all of this in mind, and they're not going to be very sympathetic to your situation if you tell them that you need more time to accept their offer because you haven't heard back on this other school's decision yet. Hopefully you see why that's unappealing to them.

What this means is that you may need to go ahead and pay a deposit at one school, knowing you might have to forfeit it down the road in order to go with your preferred school's later admit. After all, if you have one admit in hand, you'd best secure that by paying the deposit – you wouldn't want to end up with nowhere to go when the musical chairs game ends later in the season. So pay the deposit if you must. Think of it like an insurance policy. That payment ensures that you will be sitting in a bschool classroom in the fall.

Negotiating

When people are graced with multiple offers, they often start thinking about ways they can get their preferred school to sweeten the pot, to match the offer received by the other school. Many of the posts on the EssaySnark blahg in the "deciding on a school" category are focused on this sort of situation.

You're free to hit up your admissions office at the school you most want to go to, to see if they'll kick down some special deal to you to match what another school has offered – but we're doubtful that they'll agree to it.

Anyone in such a situation is typically trying to get a higher-ranked school to give them some scholarship or other free money that matches what a lesser-regarded school has offered. And that's just not how the game is usually played. The reason the lower-ranked school offered you the money in the first place was because of this exact situation: They realize that you're likely to get other offers from better-regarded schools and they're trying to entice you to accept theirs anyway.

Look at it from the perspective of the schools: Why would a higher-ranked school try to fight for you? If they were going to offer you the scholarship money, they would've offered it when they accepted it (at least, that's typically how it works).

We don't want to discourage you from trying this strategy if you have your heart set on it, but we are rather skeptical that it will pay off for you.

An MBA will increase your earnings potential significantly. An argument can easily be made than an MBA from a "better" school will increase your earnings potential more than one from a lower-ranked one. Why should the "better" school also PAY YOU for that opportunity? The math doesn't quite add up.

But go to town with your strategy – and please report back if it works! We'd love to be wrong on this one.

There are a few situations where we have seen this play out, especially if a lower-ranked school really wants you and you received a higher scholarship offer at a comparable school. Sometimes, schools at the same tier will increase an existing offer. It's rare that a higher-ranked school will.

Or, if you're in this specific situation, you might see some flexibility:

- School A accepts you, School B puts you on the waitlist.

- You pay the deposit at School A.

- Much later in the season – like, sometime after May – a higher-ranked School B accepts you off their waitlist.

You can try asking School B to offset your tuition by the amount you paid in deposit to School A. You will still need to pay a new deposit to School B; they won't waive that for you (money talks in this game, they won't hold your spot without receiving some funds). However depending on how late in the cycle it was that they accepted you, they may be more sympathetic to the fact that you had to outlay some cash at the first school, and they could cut you a small deal on it.

No guarantees on this; YMMV. Keep in mind that they have plenty of others on the waitlist who are likely clamoring for that spot that they're offering to you, so don't alienate anyone at School B if you decide to make such a request. Be polite, and remember that they do not owe you a dime. Don't forget that you're lucky they found a spot for you at all. For many people, that would be more than enough, and the previous deposit paid to School A is a small sacrifice, in the grand scheme of things, for ending up where you are. Add up the entire cost of your MBA and a throwaway deposit of a couple extra grand really doesn't matter that much. Keep the big-picture perspective in all these matters – you'll need it!

Another tip on school selection, that will help your entire MBA experience:

As you weigh the different schools' offers, continue to research and refine your career goals.

Knowing what you want to do should help you pick the school to do it at. Make sure to factor this career goals angle into much of your decision-making when you're selecting between two offers. It's not just about which school has the best international trips and more student clubs. You need to pick the school that's got the right resources to set you up for success with your post-MBA future.

Here's some "Which school?" advice posted to the EssaySnark blahg by a successful Brave Supplicant back in 2012:

```
I think it may be time to be a true future business
school student and create a nice little spreadsheet and
do some rating of what is important to me. Even if I
don't go with whatever my nifty little spreadsheet
tells me to do, I think I may gain more clarity by just
doing the exercise. If I find myself trying to rig my
system to make one school come out on top then I know
that's where I should go.
```

We've had other people tell us that they did ROI calculations too, especially when entertaining multiple offers.

What may help if you're totally stuck: Go for a walk in the woods, or to the beach if you're lucky enough to live near one. Hang out by yourself in nature for awhile. Give your time to reflect, on your own. This is indeed an important decision that you're making. It's natural to feel overwhelmed by it – but we're certain that you'll make the perfect choice for yourself!

Deferrals

While we're on the subject of which school to choose, we'll mention deferrals, which often gets tossed about as a possible strategy. Sometimes people think that they can ask one school that's admitted them for a "safety net" by hitting them up for a deferral, to move their admit from this year to next year's entering class.

This rarely works.

Some schools have a blanket "no deferrals" policy.

Others will entertain them but only on a case-by-case basis.

The situations where we've seen deferrals granted are few and far between. Here's the only cases we know of where an accepted candidate has been able to push out their matriculation for a full year:

- college senior who's been admitted to bschool but who wants to go out into the workforce for a year or so first; schools like Harvard and Stanford in particular are quite flexible with this

- military members who are called into service

- someone who's faced with a serious and unexpected illness or injury, or who has a close family member suddenly get sick or pass away (documentation may be required)

The schools don't grant deferrals for your own convenience. It's not going to work if you just recently got an amazing new job offer and you want to go do that for a year before starting your MBA. The school will almost definitely tell you that you need to cancel your acceptance and reapply next year.

Many schools are quite open to reapplicants who do this, so it's not going to negatively hurt you next time (provided it's a good reason). You are giving up your confirmed spot, though. It's not an easy decision to make but it might be the right one for you, depending on which school you've been accepted to and what your plans are now. Sometimes, it's difficult for us to get clarity on exactly what our priorities are and what our next steps should be until after we have the options solidly in hand. We understand if you had trouble deciding on what was important to you and where you wanted to go in life until you had a bschool admit locked up. It's fine to change your mind and extend your time horizons on the MBA if that's what makes the most sense for your given situation.

Or, maybe you're ready to roll with things and you're impatient to get started, ASAP – we understand that, too!

Once You've Decided on a School

Great! Now there's lots to do.

The school that accepted you likely has inundated you with information on things you need to take care of in the months to come. We're not going to try to recreate that wheel. Study that information carefully. Mark the dates and deadlines on your calendar. You can't afford to mess any of this stuff up. (One additional date you may want to track: When do you get to apply for student tickets for the school's football games? These things are important!)

We can offer up additional few tips to guide you.

Scholarships

Most schools don't need anything additional from you in order to consider you for scholarships, yet each school operates differently on this, and also on when any scholarship award will be announced. Many schools, including Chicago Booth as a prime example, will notify you of their scholarship award in real-time, during the telephone call when they're letting you know you've been accepted. Other schools, in particular Columbia and Cornell, will notify you separately, after you've been admitted, if you're being considered for a fellowship award, and then you need to go through a specific interview process. These fellowships are often awarded in the late-February timeframe at schools that handle it this way.

Other schools, such as Tuck, require a separate scholarship application essay be submitted with the main MBA application (there's a separate submission deadline for that which hits usually about a week after the round deadline).

A small number of schools separate the scholarship award from the acceptance decision entirely. Berkeley Haas requires additional essays – sometimes a lot of them – to be submitted after you're accepted if you want to be considered for the different scholarship programs available. Your school has likely informed you if you need to do anything else for the scholarship consideration part, but you may want to doublecheck that you haven't overlooked a deadline or an essay requirement in order to be in the running for this free money.

If you're lucky enough to get one of these awards, make sure you understand the complete package that you're getting. Is it an annual award, or is it for the first year of studies only? Are there any strings attached in terms of grades you need to maintain or special service you need to fulfill to the school community?

Continue to kick the tires on your career goals

You already went through an extensive career goals development process when you wrote up all those essays to pitch the schools about what you want to do with the MBA – but that was a long time ago. And the importance of having a clear grasp on your future goals still may not be understood. At most schools, recruiting for the summer internship stars *in October.* Not only will that come up fast – just a month or so after classes begin – but you won't be able to participate in all the recruiting events that you'll want to. There will inevitably be overlaps and conflicts in schedules that prevent you from attending every company's presentation.

This means, the more on-the-ground research you can do NOW, before school begins, the better positioned you'll be to take advantage of the opportunities that bschool provides.

What type of research? There's lots of things you can be doing now:

- **LinkedIn:** Research the post-MBA career paths of people in the industry(ies) you're interested in. Tap your network to see who you know who's doing the thing you want to do.

- **Informational interviews:** Connect with senior people in your target field and take them out for coffee to ask about what their work is like and what advice they have for someone transitioning in. Try to get a sense for what the job really entails. Does it match your strengths? What is life like for someone doing the day-to-day in this position? Sometimes BSers entertain unrealistic ideas of what certain jobs are about. Try to bust through the myths in your own mind so that you're an educated consumer.

- **Career Services:** Tap the schools to find out what the employment landscape looks like today. A lot will change by the time you're set to graduate in two years but there may be trends that these professionals are seeing that can help you now.

Lots of people use bschool to change careers – and lots of people totally change their minds about what careers they want to pursue, once they've started bschool. It's fine to go into the process with two totally separate ideas in mind, though you really shouldn't be considering any more than that. You'll have tremendous opportunities for learning more about different career paths once you're at school, so don't think that everything is set in stone this early. There's no problem if you change your mind from what you pitched in the essays. However, recognize that once school starts, you'll have limited time before you'll need to pick a lane and make an effort for that summer internship experience, so having the groundwork laid well in advance is going to give you an advantage.

Attend the Admit Weekend

Why? Several reasons:

- You'll want to do this if you're still deciding between multiple offers, as we mentioned above. It's a great way to get firsthand experience with the school and find out how you feel about the place. Different types of people are attracted to, and eventually admitted, to different schools. It can be surprising how different one feels from another.

- You especially want to attend Welcome Weekend if you've already decided to go to that school. You simply don't want to miss this opportunity to bond with your future classmates. If you skip Welcome Weekend, you're going to fill like the odd man out when you show up for Orientation. Everyone else will have already gotten to know each other and many of them will be networking away all through the summer. Welcome Weekend is a great opportunity to make some friends and develop some connections. And having some connections on campus is the best way to ease your transition back into the life of a student. It's stressful enough to show up on the first day to start this big adventure; it's even worse if you don't know anyone – and particularly bad if you're the only one who doesn't.

- If you've never visited campus before – or even if you have – Welcome Weekend is a chance to get to know the area and scope out neighborhoods, to figure out where you might want to live.

- While you're in town for Welcome Weekend, you can set up a mailbox at the university post office or a private maildrop (usually available for about $20/month at places like The UPS Store), and get a checking account. Establishing these specific connections to the area will make it easier for you to make the move; it's like planting seeds in your new town.

Another tip along those lines: Once you've decided on a school, set up a weather widget on your computer desktop or an app on your phone that tracks the local weather. Check in on it from time to time, to see what it's like in that area. This will help you be familiar with what to expect, climate-wise, at your future home. If you're an international student who will be coming to school in the States, you might even want to have your weather widget display the temperature in Fahrenheit, and practice converting it into Celsius – that's a great way to start getting "acclimated" (pun intended!) in advance of your actual move.

Paying your deposit

As we already mentioned, deposits are non-refundable.

However, don't hesitate to make your payment, once you know you're going there. Submitting that deposit will likely be a very empowering moment for you. It will make everything about going to bschool more "real" - most people feel pretty darned good when they do it (unlike most other times when we have to fork over a chunk of change like that!).

Keep in mind that some schools (Duke is one) will not accept credit cards for any deposits or tuition payments, so you may need to send in a check, or arrange for a wire transfer (usually about a $25 fee from your bank). Read their instructions carefully.

Once you've paid your deposit at the school you're going to, then it's considered polite to remove yourself from the other schools' lists of active admits. In other words: If you've been admitted to several schools, let those other schools know once you've committed to the one school you'll be attending. That way, they can make arrangements to let in someone else to take the spot that they'd been holding for you. It doesn't make any sense for you to hang on to your admission at schools you know you won't be going to.

The background check

This is cause for concern for many — but it needn't be. If you didn't lie on your application, you're going to be fine with the background check process. The level of scrutiny that admitted students go through is no worse than what someone applying to be a barrista at Starbucks would be subject to. If you don't think you could land a barrista job, based on inconsistencies and oddities lurking in your past, well...

There are two main companies that do this, Kroll and Re Vera Services. Even if your school uses Kroll, you might want to read the Re Vera FAQ (http://reveraservices.com/FAQ.html) to increase your comfort level with how it works (Kroll seems not to have much information publicly available). Both services have slightly different procedures, and each school has different requirements, so we're not going to offer a definitive description of literally what you'll go through.

The general protocol is that the verification service will make sure that the data you entered in your application is accurate. They will probably contact your recommenders and your employers.

Which means: If you haven't notified your employer about the whole bschool thing, well.... you'll need to do so soon. Obviously you don't want the news that you're headed to bschool to come from anyone but yourself. You can get the background check started and ask that they hold off on contacting your current employer until you notify them that it's OK, but you really need to resolve this ASAP.

Most schools are reasonably flexible about this process and they say that you only need to have it done before orientation – but you wouldn't want August to roll around, and you've relocated to your new apartment in your new city, and you still have this important thing hanging over your head. You should at least start the background check process as soon as you can. Some schools have deadlines by which you must begin the process (e.g., May 1st for NYU). It typically only takes a week or so to move through all the steps.

But the background check people might ask you for documentation – including old employment records like W2s or tax returns. You probably aren't planning on moving all those dusty old files with you to your new home. Get the background check done as early as possible – well before you start packing up your life and putting stuff in storage.

Small variations in the data that you reported in the application and the records of your past employer are fine, and even to be expected. However, if the background check turns up a significant discrepancy, all schools reserve the right to rescind an offer of acceptance or even kick someone out of school if they don't catch it until after the term has already started. We assume that you didn't lie on your application and so it will not be an issue for you to pass the background check.

Don't forget your manners

We'll wrap up this first section with a gentle reminder: Did you thank your recommenders? Now that you've been accepted to a top MBA program, it would be appropriate to offer them a little gesture of appreciation. Depending on who they are / your relationship to them, you might consider getting them a box of chocolate, or a bottle of wine, or even taking them out to dinner. A nice card is always appropriate.

While we're on this topic, we'll also mention that you'll want to navigate your exit from your current company carefully. Beginnings and endings are important; these are moments that you'll remember, and you always want to treat people well and leave on good terms. It's a small world, and especially in certain industries, your reputation is all that you have. Stay on good terms with people, put in an honest day's work for every day you get paid (no coasting), and leave things in a better condition than you found them. That's a great formula for a life of no regrets.

Speaking of which:

Important and FUN! Decisions

You've probably already started dreaming about when you're going to resign from your job. Maybe your boss and everyone at work knows that you've been accepted to bschool, and they have been celebrating right along with you. Maybe they've already asked you this important question point-blank and you committed to staying through the summer. Or maybe you've kept your bschool plans a secret till now, and you're starting to wonder about how and when you'll break the news.

We have some advice for you to consider as you work through these important decisions and identify the milestones on the timeline of now till bschool orientation.

Let's work backwards.

Assuming that your bschool experience will start sometime in August, then that's your drop-dead date for when you have to be on campus. However, EssaySnark recommends that you plan to relocate much earlier than that – *especially* if you're relocating from overseas, and even more especially if you've never lived in the US or any other Western country before. You need time to make this transition.

When should you move?

Our advice? Plan to fly in at least **one month** before your first formal on-campus activity begins.

- For most students, that would be Orientation, which is a week or so before the fall semester formally starts. This is in early to mid August for many American programs.

- Some students take advantage of Summer Start or Language School or Math Camp or other such pre-MBA on-campus programs offered by the school. These typically happen in July.

If you don't have housing arrangements already, then you definitely want to allow for a month before the formal school programs begin. Finding an affordable place to live in some towns like Charlottesville (Darden) or Durham (Duke) is not so difficult; it can be incredibly stressful in places like New York City (NYU and Columbia) or California (UCLA, Berkeley-Haas and Stanford).

If you are relocating with a partner or a family, then we recommend arriving in your new town six weeks ahead of school start if you can pull it off. You want to give your family as much of *your time* as possible to help them settle in. They're not going to see very much of you once your formal school program begins, so it will help them tremendously if you can be there for their own new-city/new-culture adjustment period. The first few months in a new place can be very rough on anyone. Make it as easy as possible on the people you care about by building in a buffer zone around the relocation process. Move early if you can.

So that means, you're probably going to be moving in the middle of the summer.

When should you resign from your job?

You should plan to quit your job at least a week before your departure date; two weeks ahead of time would be better. If you've never done a significant move like this before then you may not realize how much there is to do right before you leave for your new home. Not only will you need to box up your things and pack your suitcase, and moving out of your apartment and canceling the utilities and possibly even selling your car, but there will likely be many people who want to wish you well with bon voyage parties and the like; it's quite possible that your last few days will be jam-packed and chaotic.

Side note: If you're planning on shipping things from overseas to your new home at bschool, expect them to take at least four weeks to arrive – and possibly much longer. The minimum that a coast-to-coast mover is likely to require to get your stuff there when shipping within the US is around two weeks. Plan accordingly.

Anyway, we're betting that once you got the news that you were admitted to bschool, a part of you quit caring about your job. Let's face it, that's a common reaction. It's hard to stay engaged when you've got one foot out the door – especially since it's quite likely that your dissatisfaction with your current job is a main reason why you applied to bschool in the first place.

Because of this and the sense of wanderlust that sets in, many people choose to resign much earlier, and they use their newfound freedom to do some adventure travel. Most MBA programs have organized first-year treks, such as the Kellogg Kwest program, Ross' M-Trek, and Booth Random Walk. These are excellent opportunities to meet your future classmates and get some bonding in early. Plus, they're often to exotic locales – they can be very special experiences indeed. If you have the budget for it, we strongly suggest that you take advantage of these trips. Or, plan one of your own.

The pre-matriculation *not-yet-a-bschool-student-but-close* period during the spring and summer before your MBA program begins is a specific and wonderful phase in life that you probably will never experience again: You have a major big thing looming on the horizon but it hasn't started yet, and the responsibilities of your past life are dropping away... there's a sense of freedom and potential in this time that is just amazing. We strongly recommend that you make the most of it! Plan something fun. You won't get another chance like this, possibly ever (a honeymoon after getting married has a little bit of this flavor, but that typically lasts only a few weeks, and many of you have already done that!).

How should you resign?

If the people at work don't yet know you're headed to bschool and you managed to keep it a secret throughout the process of interview invites and decisions coming out even though you were checking your email frantically for hours on end and getting no work at all done during those times, then you need to handle the delivery of your departure news carefully. It's likely to irritate some people if you simply spring it on them in the manner of, "Oh by the way I'm leaving in two weeks" - some people may feel betrayed, that you were working on these big plans for yourself and never breathed a word of it. It can be especially complicated if you've been recently assigned to a plum project or got a big promotion or a raise. Be sensitive to these issues when you plan your announcement. There's been people who have gone to bat for you at your company, probably, who have vouched for you and maybe even recommended you for your current role, who will be a little vulnerable in the overall organization when news comes out that you have sprung this on them.

The other potential complication is that the background check process typically requires that your current employer be contacted for verification. You clearly don't want your company to be notified about your imminent departure through a procedure like that. If you're not ready to inform your manager, then be sure to have your background check put on an "employer hold" (Re Vera Services allows for this and hopefully Kroll does too). Or, to make sure that there won't be any possibility of crossed wires, wait to initiate the background check until after you have informed your manager.

We're assuming that you've resigned from a company before, so we won't go into what to say in a letter and all of that. Our basic advice is, write up your formal resignation letter, addressed to your current direct supervisor. Include today's date, and specify your intended last date of employment. Let them know that you can be flexible, if you can be. Even though two weeks notice is considered standard, in this case, give your notification as far in advance as you possibly can. The formal letter should be short and sweet. You don't have to go into the reasons behind your departure, though you can do so if you like. Keep a copy for your personal records.

Then, schedule a meeting with your boss, or ask to take her out for coffee. Try to do this at a time when you know she won't be frazzled; in other words, if you work for the CEO and there's a board meeting coming up, wait until after that's over before you plan your big announcement.

Go into the meeting with a plan. Map out the projects and deliverables that you have pending and offer details to your manager of how you intend to get everything done. Come up with ideas for who you can transition your tasks to. Be proactive in helping to offload your duties. If you know someone who might be a good fit for you job that you can recommend into the company, then take the extra step of getting their resume ahead of time if you can. Make your manager feel comfortable that this is not going to be a major upheaval to her life.

Don't tell anyone at the company before you tell your boss. Even though you may swear your buddy to secrecy, once you've told someone then you have lost all control over the information, and the risk is too great that the news will fly around without you being the one who's telling it. Resist the urge. Be an adult and deal with the person who needs to know the most, first. Then you can share the news with your friends on the team.

Leaving on good terms means not just not burning bridges; it means making your departure as smooth and painless as possible to those who will be most affected by it.

How will you find an apartment?

We already made the suggestion that attending Welcome Weekend can be helpful in allowing you time to get familiar with the area where you will be living. You could also potentially hook up with a roommate at that time, if you're interested in sharing a space to keep expenses down. You might even consider extending that trip for Welcome Weekend by an extra day or so to do some apartment hunting. Keep in mind that the apartments around any university are likely to have a lot of vacancies in the late May/early June timeperiod, since that's when many students are graduating and moving away. You may find the best availability then.

Your school will of course have lots of resources to help you with the housing search. Craig's List (www.craigslist.org) is a great site to try for rentals in many cities. Be careful about enlisting the help of a local realtor; in many cities, the person doing the renting – that is, *you* – is on the hook for a significant fee when a realtor handles the transaction. In other cities, the landlord pays the fee. Find out in advance what the rules and laws are in the city you're moving to.

You can do some legwork in front of your computer. Use Google Maps StreetView to check out the neighborhoods of possible apartments. Recommendations from current students is the best way to go in deciding where to live. You want to be close to campus, given how much time you'll be spending there. You should also check out the relative convenience of public transportation. In some cities, the less expensive housing units are ones that are quite far away from where you need to be, so it's a tradeoff that must be carefully considered.

Will you need a car?

If you're relocating to another city somewhere in the same country where you currently live, then maybe you can just drive your existing car to bschool and you're set.

If you're moving from somewhere far away, you may be wondering what you should do about the car situation.

In most cases, you won't need a car at bschool – at least, you won't need one right away, if you need one at all. In fact, if you're headed to school in New York or in another big city (Berkeley or LA or Chicago), a car could be a liability. Parking is often hard to come by and very expensive in the city, and having a car can turn out to be way more hassle than it's worth. (Just ask anyone who owns a car in Manhattan about "alternate side of the street parking" and you'll get an earful.) EssaySnark recommends sitting on the question of whether you need a car or not. Ask around with the current students at every opportunity, and see what they say. In most cases, you'll survive just fine for awhile in your first weeks at bschool, and you can decide later how you feel about being wheel-less and whether it cramps your style too much. Most people spend massive amounts of time on campus every single day and there won't be that many opportunities for you to be using your car anyway.

That being said: If you're attending a school like Columbia where few people have cars, and you do have one, you'll find yourself suddenly very popular on the weekends, when everyone wants to get out of town. It might have its advantages to have one!

Of course, if you plan on buying a car, you probably need to get a driver's license.

Do you need a new state driver's license?

If you're not going to have a car at bschool, then maybe not – but it wouldn't hurt to have a valid American license anyway if you're an international student. At least, some states would require one. Others allow international students to drive on the license issued by their home countries, though an International Driver's Permit is often also needed. As you can see, the laws actually vary quite a bit from state to state. Since we don't want to give bum advice on this, we need to direct you to the Department of Motor Vehicles for the state you're moving to. In most cases, you will need a social security number to apply for a driver's license; once you are granted your student visa (typically a F-1) you will qualify to get the SSN.

If you're a US citizen, you may want to get a driver's license from your new state's Department of Motor Vehicles as soon as you move there, as a way to establish residency – which may qualify you for the lower in-state tuition at schools like UC-Berkeley, UCLA, and Michigan Ross in the second year of your MBA. Students on immigrant visas do not qualify for residency and so this does not apply to them.

There's lots of opportunity for road trips and weekend adventures, and it will prevent some possible hiccups in renting a car if you have a domestic driver's license (you'll need a major credit card as well for that).

Financial Preparations

We already touched on this at the very beginning of this *Guide* but let's go into more details now. As we said earlier, you need to get real about how much money you'll need to live on during school – and you'll need to get used to not having an income.

In recent years, many bschools have started asking questions right upfront, in the online applications, about how applicants intend to fund the MBA. This change in protocol is due to the unfortunately very common situation where someone is admitted to bschool and then realizes how expensive it really is, and they end up backing out of the whole idea. That's an inconvenience to everyone and the schools want to avoid the problems with sticker shock that unprepared admits may face.

Every school lists their Costs of Attendance figures on their websites. As a very rough generalization, you can expect you'll need about $80,000 minimum per year at an average school – though be warned: the estimate runs to $95,000 for a school like Columbia. These figures obviously increase significantly if there is a wife and/or children in the picture.

Add in a bunch more if you're planning on ever going home to visit your parents for holidays, or if you're planning on actually participating in any of those international experiences that you told the adcom you wanted to participate in, when you wrote your application essays. Travel for those are on your dime (there are some exceptions with residencies built into some "global" programs like the Duke Cross-Continent or Darden GEMBA and other Executive MBAs, where housing and meals are included for the on-campus segments, though airfare and ground transportation costs typically are not).

So yeah; $85k+. That sounds daunting. What can you do to prepare?

First, start stashing your cash. As we encouraged you at the beginning of this *Guide*, pay down any credit card debt you've accumulated, and then begin to build your savings.

Next, recognize that bschool students are considered very good risks by lenders. It's fairly easy to qualify for loans for a significant chunk of your MBA education – up to 90% being quite common. This is because you're seen as a good bet: Most MBA grads make a very nice salary coming out, and they're easily able to pay off the loans. Of course, you need to have a decent (and clean) credit history if you're going to get a decent interest rate. If you don't, then the rate may be much higher, or you may need a co-signer (usually a parent or spouse with good credit and a regular income) to help out in getting approved.

Many bschools – but not all – have partnerships with lenders whereby international students can get loans without a US co-signer. If you're an international student then hopefully you looked into these issues ahead of time. We've had cases where a Brave Supplicant we were working with chose not to even apply to a school based on the lending packages available.

All schools have support for students through the financial aid office. That's the first place to begin. International students are often advised to seek out loans (and scholarships) from their home country as the first opportunity.

What will make the loan application process easier?

1. If your credit report is clean – thus, the advice offered earlier, to pull a copy of your report and inspect it.

2. If your financial situation is in order – thus, the advice offered earlier, to pay down credit card debt and if possible, find out your FICO score, so you know what you're dealing with (a "good" score is 700 or above, and anything below a 600 is moving into trouble territory – hmmm... sounds like the GMAT!). If your FICO score is lower, it's usually not too difficult to raise it through good credit management practices such as reducing the amount of credit being utilized, and never being late with your payments, among other steps, though note that it does take some time for significant changes to be reflected in the number.

3. US citizens and residents will also need their last-year's federal tax return, so get your taxes done as soon as possible in the new year.

Why is all this important to be working on now, even if you won't be headed to bschool for many many months? Well, because these are big issues for many people to tackle. This may be the most significant investment you've made to date; it's not trivial.

And, for foreign students, this is very important (*very very* important): The US government will not issue a student visa unless they are assured that the applicant can pay for his or her education. This needs to be documented, with proof of your liquid assets and financial resources or sponsoring organization's commitment presented to the Visa Officer when you go for your interview.

A caution: Be conservative about applying for any new credit – of any type – before you get your student loan approved. Now is not the time to go buy a new car or sign up for a timeshare or something. Every time you apply for credit, it hits your credit report as a "pull", and too many of those start to have a negative drag on your FICO score. While it might make sense to get a new credit card now, while you're still gainfully employed and it's easier to qualify, you should plan things carefully so that you don't accidentally clobber your credit right at the time when you need to be boosting it.

EssaySnark is no expert in all of these things, so seek out the help of those who know more if you're having trouble with your strategies. Our goal with this is to simply alert you to the different issues that may play a part in your approval process, and to encourage you to get started on the financial planning aspects right away.

We also encourage you to begin tracking your expenses. Having an awareness of what it costs to maintain your current standard of living is important. Identify the amenities that are mandatory, and those that you've gotten accustomed to based on your current salary but which you may be able to live without for a year or so.

You might even want to go on a "financial fast" where you live for a week or two with spending only on the bare essentials (rent, utilities, groceries for home-cooked meals, etc.). Cash only. No credit card charges allowed. (Here's a website to teach you the concepts: https://www.rebelmouse.com/financialfast/) This will get you in the mindset of what it's going to be like as an MBA student, and it may motivate you to sock away more money than you otherwise would. Assuming you go for the standard summer MBA internship, you'll have a salary for a couple months next year, but it won't put a major dent into the red ink that will be flowing from your bschool budget.

Starting to examine your financial situation and figuring out how you're going to cover these costs is critical to moving through the process of getting your butt seated in the MBA classroom in August. You got accepted to bschool which was the hardest part! Now you just need to work through the details of financing. Don't freak out; your school's financial aid office will help you.

International Preparations

If you're an American headed to a US school, you may be tempted to skip this part – but don't.

The modern bschool experience is nothing if not international. If you're going for your MBA, there's a high probability that you'll have some foreign travel in your future. And of course if you're coming to the States as an international student, then there's plenty of ways you need to prepare for that.

The most basic – whether you're American or not – is that you need a passport.

You have a passport, right? Of course you do. But is it ready to accompany you on all your bschool adventures?

Go dig it out. Right now. And look at it. What's the expiration date?

Passports

If you're a foreign student coming to the US, your passport will need to be valid for at least six months beyond the end of your educational program when you'll be leaving the country. If you're an American, we recommend the same: six months past the end of the MBA.

You have more free time now than you will when you're in school. Believe us, you will be chaotically busy while studying for your MBA. Renewing a soon-to-be-expired passport is not the type of thing you want to have to worry about – and it would totally suck if you discovered too late that it was expired.

Here's a few other points to check on now:

- You also need to make sure that there are enough blank pages in your passport to accommodate travel. As an example, if you're an American who wants to go on a student trip to India, you'll need at least two full blank pages for the visa to be affixed into your passport.

- If you're a foreign student coming to the US, make sure that the name that the school has on its documents is an exact match to the name in your passport. If there are any discrepancies, it can delay or prevent your student visa approval process.

This goes for any partners and children who may be accompanying you to bschool – or boyfriends or girlfriends who you will want to visit you while you're there. Do an audit of everyone's passport situation and make sure that the details are dealt with now, while you have the luxury of time to handle such things.

If your passport is due to expire soon, or if you don't have enough blank pages, deal with it with the State Department now.

Immunizations

There are no vaccination requirements for foreigners traveling to the US, however many business schools do require proof of vaccination before you can begin classes. These typically include vaccinations for measles, mumps, and rubella (sometimes abbreviated as "MMR"), and also meningitis. You'll either need to submit proof that you've had these shots, or at some schools, you can have a blood test that will identify whether or not you've been immunized. Your school will let you know the requirements. This is yet another piece of paper that you need to locate and submit, so it's one more thing you'll want to take care of before packing up your stuff for the move.

If you're an international student, find your immunization records.

Locate your birth certificate, too.

You may need these documents in the US.

If you're an American who's planning on traveling abroad during your studies, you may need some vaccinations before you depart. The Center for Disease Control and the State Department websites lists recommended vaccinations by region of the world (e.g., Hepatitis A vaccinations are recommended before traveling to places like Thailand). Some of these vaccinations must be delivered in a series of shots over time, so again, planning ahead and knowing what to expect is important.

International Student Visa

Getting a US student visa is easy, and the London Business School admissions people say that it's easy in the UK, too. Here's a post from LBS about this from January 2014:

http://blog.admissions.london.edu/2014/01/23/studying-and-working-in-the-uk/

We don't have any experience with that so we'll discuss only the US process here – but this should go smoothly for you, regardless of which country you'll be entering for school, as long as you pay attention to the requirements and give the government immigration agency what they need.

You will need to prepare your materials carefully; the US consulate officer will examine them closely for evidence of fraud. But if you managed to get into a good MBA program then we're betting you can handle this part too! Just double-check everything; any mistakes could cause problems. As with many other aspects of your business school preparations, the admissions office will guide you on what you need and what to expect.

Note: You don't need to pay anyone to help you get your student visa! Please avoid those services that claim to do it for you. This is a straightforward process. Just pay attention to the details and you'll be fine.

The US consulate in your country will want to see a lot of documents as part of your student visa application, including transcripts from college and your offer letter from your accepting school. Believe it or not, they'll even want your GMAT score report. This is to make sure that you're a legitimate student who's really been accepted to school. They are evaluating you to issue a non-immigrant visa, meaning they want to see proof that you intend to come to the States only for a time, and then return to your home country.

As an example, the Visa Officer might ask you about the school you're going to – why did you apply there, what do you know about it, etc. Also career goals. Basically, all that school research that you did as part of your original application process will help you now, too (who knew?).

Our best advice? Simply be honest with the Visa Officer. Even though you'll be telling the truth about your application, you still may want to practice for the interview – only because you're likely to be a little nervous. (Note: This is an interview that you don't have to wear a suit for.) These are government officials and they tend not to be the friendliest types; don't be surprised if your interviewer doesn't even crack a smile. And don't joke around with them. Take it seriously and go in with a professional demeanor, and it'll likely be over in a hot second and you'll be on your way with the approved application.

Most bschool students get an F-1 visa. Under the U.S. Optional Practical Training (OPT) immigrant program, you can apply to be allowed to work in the U.S. for one year – which covers your summer internship, and can help an American employer to bring you on board after you graduate, since you'll be legal to work right away without additional processing needed from them. From there, the employer can process you as an H1-B visa candidate, which should be straightforward for them based on how you will be classified. Again, consult your school's International Students Office for guidance on this and all other issues.

Tip: Once you get the visa, scan all your documents and store them digitally (password-protected), then keep multiple copies in different places, including some in your home country with your parents or someone you trust, in case you need to be able to retrieve them unexpectedly.

After you get the visa approved, you can apply for a social security number. You'll need the SSN for many things while living in the US, including getting a bank account, a credit card, and a cell phone plan.

Cultural Issues

If you're a foreigner who's never lived in the US before – and especially if you've never even visited – then be prepared for some culture shock. Even if you're in love with America, it doesn't matter; you will inevitably feel homesick and even somewhat miserable at some point in your first few months in the States.

And, you need to get used to doing things all these different ways:

- Our currency is confusing. The coins are not sized proportional to value.

- Our temperatures are confusing. The Fahrenheit system doesn't make any sense to someone who's used to Celsius.

- Our measurements are confusing. Inches, feet, and miles are not logical (unlike centimeters, meters, and kilometers).

- Our customs are confusing. Shaking hands on greeting and direct eye contact are expected, but standing too close is not. (Americans need personal space.)

If you're unused to any of these things – if you've never spent significant time in a Western country – then you'll want to prepare yourself. A great way to do so is this video series from the international students at Columbia Business School: http://youtu.be/tPfB6GIjM9Q

Get familiar with the foreign customs. If you're an American who will be attending school overseas, this is just as important for you. We've heard that Americans headed to the UK have just as much culture shock and homesickness as foreigners who come to the US, even though the language is (ostensibly) the same.

Also remember that the cultural norms extend to the classroom.

No matter which school you're attending – HBS or elsewhere – you will be expected to actively participate in the classroom.

American learning styles and customs are different. It's not about rote memorization; it's about active learning, and being engaged and even proactive during class time. This may take some getting used to for those coming from different educational systems – and if English is not your first language, it may be intimidating to speak in front of the class. Don't worry; it will get easier over time! But also, don't space out during class – you have to always be paying attention! Being cold-called when you're daydreaming sucks pretty back. ☺

Academic Preparations

Here's the part that you may be least enthused about: You need to be honest with yourself, whether you're ready for bschool or not.

Did you struggle with the quant section on the GMAT? Like, did you end up with a score lower than 70th percentile on the math part? Or lower than 650 overall? Or did you score poorly on Integrated Reasoning, such as a 4 or below? If any of these are true, then please recognize the challenges. We strongly encourage you to do some advance academic prep. You really must take action – before you arrive on campus.

The hardest part of getting the MBA is still ahead of you. Many Brave Supplicants are quant geniuses and had no trouble with the math side of things. But not all of you are. If math isn't your strong suit, then you need to get comfortable with it ahead of time, or you're setting yourself up to be miserable.

As one of our former BSer-people wrote to us at the end of their first semester:

"I underestimated how steep the learning curve would be."

This person was having so many challenges that they were even thinking about quitting. Yes, it can be that bad if you're not ready for it.

The first semester at a top MBA program is GRUELING. Not only are you getting back in the habit of studying and taking tests, but the pace is intense. You'll be behind in your assignments practically on the first day. There's always way more reading than you can ever hope to complete. And the simple fact of the matter is, this is *graduate school.*

That fact completely escaped the 'Snark when we were headed into our first days of our MBA classes. This is not a continuation of college. This is harder.

The teachers all assume that you have at least a passing knowledge of the material. This is going to be true in many of the classes – but it's especially true in statistics, micro- and macroeconomics, and accounting. Most of your colleagues in those classes will in fact have taken at least one course in college on those subjects. If you have not, then you are going to be giving yourself a massive gift if you spend time now in learning about them.

You don't have to pre-take a class that you're going to be taking in bschool. But it would be a great idea if you would become familiar with the basics.

If your bschool offers a pre-term MBA prep course, either online or in person, then you definitely should take advantage of it if you're nervous about being prepared for these subjects. Schools like NYU and their Summer Start and Duke with its Summer Math Review and Language Institute offer big advantages to students, to help them hit the ground running on their first full day of the actual MBA curriculum. Not all schools offer these programs though; we've heard that Kellogg is rather deficient in the amount of support they provide to non-traditionals. Which is disturbing, given how many of them they admit.

A variety of commercial programs have sprung up to serve the needs of pre-MBA people. We can't vouch for any of these but they might be worth looking into. The ones that have come across our radar include MBA IQ, MBA Math, and MBA Day Camp. If you take any of those courses, then we'd love to hear your opinion on them, whether they're worth it or not. We have literally never heard of anyone who's gone through them so your feedback would be useful for us in knowing what to recommend to others in the future.

You don't need to go through a formal training though. You could easily design your own pre-MBA training using the resources listed out at the Duke MBA Ready website, offered up for the EMBA students:

http://www.fuqua.duke.edu/student_resources/mba_ready_executive/

The only risk with that is, knowing what we know about people like you and how much you procrastinate, you may not ever get it done.

But if you want to give it a shot, here's the bare-bones basics of what you'll need to know:

- Math skills – college-level calculus

- Microsoft Excel – you need to know how to write a formula in a cell

- Microsoft PowerPoint – you should be able to create a decent-looking slide

For another opinion on this from a much more esteemed expert, check out this (very very long) transcription of a speech by Charlie Munger, who as you hopefully know is Warren Buffett's partner at Berkshire Hathaway, otherwise known as a Super Successful and Seriously Smart Guy:

http://ycombinator.com/munger.html

The tl;dr of it is, you need to know *mental models* in order to be a successful investor (or businessperson). These include high school algebra, accounting, statistics, microeconomics. You don't need to be an expert in any of these things but they need to be familiar. If you're interested in investment management, we recommend you stick with it and read through that whole speech. Interesting insights, if you ask us.

Finally, in terms of academic preparation, we will leave you with this:

You should be prepared to work 50 to 60 hours per week in bschool.

Come to campus, ready to go. It's going to be exhilarating, and exhausting. And you'll probably love every minute of it.

But you're more likely to love it if you're ready.

What to Do Next

Get busy!

Former Brave Supplicant, now Soon-To-Be-Bschool-Student, we applaud you! You made it through the very difficult admissions process and you've been accepted. That's at least half the battle!

Now you need to work through a vast array of logistics and bureaucratic challenges to get yourself situated before bschool begins. We wish you the very best with it, and we hope this little *Guide* has given you a lay-of-the-land overview that helps you with all the to-do lists and project planning that you'll need to undertake. Lots of details to keep track of — but you got admitted into bschool so we know you're up for it!

We hope you're still reading the EssaySnark blahg at essaysnark.com and we invite any questions, comments, corrections or other feedback that you may want to offer up. The next crop of Brave Supplicants coming along would surely appreciate hearing your advice! You can drop us an email at gethelpnow@essaysnark.com (or find EssaySnark on Twitter) if you have anything to add.

We wish you luck on your MBA adventure!

FOLLOW ESSAYSNARK ON TWITTER!

"Try not to become a man of success, but rather try to become a man of value."

Albert Einstein